I Love Myself More

How to Master Self-Love to Attract Success and Happiness

Amelia Vazquez

Copyright © 2025 All rights reserved.

First published by Amelia Vazquez 2025

All rights reserved. No part of this publication may be reproduced, stored or transmitted in any form or by any means, electronic, mechanical, photocopying, recording, scanning, or otherwise without written permission from the publisher. It is illegal to copy this book, post it to a website, or distribute it by any other means without permission.

First edition

Dedication

This book is dedicated to everyone on the journey of learning to love themselves — you are worthy, you are enough, and you are limitless.

Table of Contents

Introduction

Chapter 1 Appreciation of Oneself

Chapter 2 The Roots of Low Self-Worth

Chapter 3 Love and Respect Yourself

Chapter 4 Live Intentionally

Chapter 5 Forgive Yourself

Chapter 6 Let go

Chapter 7 Take your Power Back

Introduction

The Moment Everything Changed

I remember the exact moment I realized I didn't love myself.

I was sitting in my car, parked in front of a place I didn't even want to be — a job that drained me, surrounded by people who didn't value me, living a life that felt like it belonged to someone else. I had makeup on, a smile painted across my lips, but inside? I was exhausted. Not just tired — *emotionally bankrupt*. I had spent so much of my life chasing love, validation, approval... and still felt invisible.

That day, I looked at myself in the mirror and saw a stranger.
A woman who said yes when she wanted to scream no.
A woman who twisted herself to be what others wanted — and lost her magic along the way.
A woman who thought love had to be earned.

But something shifted. It wasn't loud or dramatic. It was quiet, like a whisper from deep within:
"You can choose you."

At first, I didn't know what that meant. How do you "choose yourself" when you've been conditioned to believe your worth is tied to productivity, appearance, or someone else's approval? But that tiny spark inside me wouldn't go out. I began doing something radical — I started listening to *myself*.

I asked myself what I wanted. What I needed. What I deserved.
And for the first time, I answered honestly.

Self-love didn't come overnight. It came in small, sacred moments.
When I said no and didn't explain myself.
When I walked away from what didn't feel right.
When I looked in the mirror and chose compassion over criticism.

And slowly… everything began to shift.
Opportunities opened. Relationships healed or fell away.
I no longer begged to be chosen — because I had already chosen *me*.
Success stopped feeling like a distant mountain and started showing up naturally, because I was no longer fighting against my own worth.

This book isn't about perfection. It's about power. **The power of loving yourself so deeply, so unapologetically, that the world has no choice but to rise up and meet you there.**

If you're tired of settling, shrinking, or forgetting who you are — I wrote this for you.
Because once you fall in love with yourself, everything else aligns.

Welcome to the beginning of your becoming.

Chapter 1: Appreciation of Oneself

I never imagined that a single moment could unravel everything I thought I knew about myself. But there I was, standing in the middle of my apartment, surrounded by the remnants of a life I had meticulously built around someone else. The silence was deafening, broken only by the ticking of the clock and the distant hum of city life outside my window.

Just days before, my world had seemed complete. I was in a relationship that, on the surface, appeared perfect. We shared dreams, laughter, and plans for the future. But beneath the facade, I had been slowly losing pieces of myself—compromising, adjusting, and silencing my own needs to keep the peace.

The breakup was sudden, a culmination of unspoken tensions and ignored red flags. As he walked out the door, taking with him the illusion of our shared future, I felt an overwhelming emptiness. But amidst the pain, a quiet realization began to surface: I had been neglecting the most important relationship of all—the one with myself.

In the days that followed, I embarked on a journey inward. I began to reflect on the choices that led me to this point, recognizing patterns of self-neglect and a deep-seated belief that I needed to earn love by diminishing myself. It was a painful truth to confront, but it was also liberating.

This wake-up call was not just about the end of a relationship; it was about the beginning of a new chapter—one where I would learn to prioritize my own well-being, set healthy boundaries, and rediscover the joy of being in my own company.

Through journaling, therapy, and moments of solitude, I started to rebuild my sense of self. I explored activities that brought me joy, reconnected with friends who uplifted me, and most importantly, I began to speak to myself with kindness and compassion.

This journey wasn't linear. There were setbacks and moments of doubt. But with each step, I grew stronger and more aligned with my true self. I learned that self-love isn't about perfection; it's about acceptance, resilience, and the courage to honor one's own needs and desires.

As I embraced this newfound self-love, I noticed a shift in my external world. Opportunities that once seemed out of reach began to present themselves. Relationships became more authentic, and I attracted connections that resonated with my values.

This transformation taught me that when we love ourselves deeply and unapologetically, we create a foundation for genuine happiness and success. We become magnets for experiences that reflect our inner worth.

In the chapters that follow, I will share the tools, insights, and practices that supported me on this journey. My hope is that by sharing my story, you will feel empowered to embark on your own path of self-discovery and embrace the incredible person that you are.

Remember, the most profound love story you'll ever experience is the one you have with yourself. Let this be your wake-up call.

here is something profoundly beautiful about sitting with yourself — not to judge, not to fix, but simply to *know*.

Most of us go through life being more familiar with what others expect from us than what we truly desire. We wear masks. We mold ourselves into what we think will be accepted, loved, or praised. And in doing so, we drift further and further from the one person we should know more intimately than anyone else: *ourselves.*

But here's the truth — the more you come home to yourself, the more you'll see just how extraordinary you really are.

Getting to know yourself isn't always easy. It takes courage to look inward. To ask the deeper questions:
What makes me feel alive?
What do I need in this season of my life?
What are my fears, my dreams, my boundaries, my gifts?

But as you explore these questions, something magical happens.

You begin to peel back the layers — not to become someone new, but to uncover the real you beneath the noise. You begin to recognize patterns, reclaim lost parts of yourself, and rediscover passions you had buried to please others. You realize that you are not "too much" or "not enough" — you are *exactly right* in your essence.

With understanding comes appreciation. You'll start to admire your own resilience, your sensitivity, your quirks, your strength. You'll stop comparing yourself to others because you'll see that what makes you different is what makes you powerful. There is no one else on this planet with your exact blend of thoughts, energy, intuition, and heart.

And when you begin to truly see yourself — not the version you've been told to be, but the woman you *are* — you start to *respect* yourself.

Respect transforms everything. It shows up in how you speak to yourself, in the boundaries you set, in the standards you raise, and in the spaces you choose to enter. You stop settling. You stop chasing. You stop shrinking to fit into boxes you were never meant to fit in.

Getting to know yourself is the foundation of deep, lasting self-love. It's the sacred relationship that fuels all others. Because when you fully embrace who you are — you no longer seek permission to be her.

Accept Yourself

Self-acceptance is one of the most powerful and liberating acts of love we can offer ourselves. And yet, it is often one of the most difficult.

For years, many of us carry an invisible weight — the pressure to be someone else: more successful, more attractive, more likable, more accomplished. We place conditions on our self-worth, convincing ourselves that only when we reach a certain milestone or become a "better version" of ourselves will we finally be deserving of love, respect, and happiness.

But this mindset only fuels self-rejection. It causes us to live in a constant state of inadequacy, measuring our value through the lens of others' expectations and ideals we were never meant to fulfill.

True growth begins not with striving, but with **acceptance**.

The Meaning of Acceptance

To accept oneself is not to settle or stop growing — rather, it is the foundation upon which meaningful growth is built. Acceptance is the courageous decision to recognize your whole self — your strengths and your struggles, your light and your shadows — and to hold space for all of it without shame or judgment.

It is the recognition that you are not broken, flawed, or behind. You are a human being, worthy of love, respect, and compassion — right now, as you are.

Acceptance does not mean ignoring areas of improvement or dismissing personal responsibility. Instead, it means releasing the toxic belief that you must *earn* your worth. It is choosing to see yourself as *enough*, while still aspiring to grow in ways that feel aligned with your values and purpose.

The Freedom of Embracing Your Whole Self

There is profound freedom that comes with radical self-acceptance. When you stop fighting who you are, you reclaim the energy once spent on hiding, performing, or striving for external validation. You are able to stand in your authenticity without apology. You begin to make choices from a place of self-respect, not self-doubt.

With self-acceptance, comparison fades. You no longer feel threatened by the success or opinions of others, because you trust in your own path. You recognize that your value does not depend on how you measure up to anyone else — it is inherent, constant, and unwavering.

Honoring Your Story

Part of accepting yourself is learning to embrace your story — all of it. This includes the moments of pain, failure, and regret. Instead of viewing these experiences as sources of shame, you begin to understand them as essential chapters in the journey that shaped your resilience and wisdom.

To accept yourself is to offer yourself the grace you so freely give to others. It is the daily decision to speak kindly to yourself, to forgive your past missteps, and to see your reflection not through a lens of criticism, but of compassion.

A New Foundation

When you operate from a place of self-acceptance, everything changes. Your relationships become more genuine, your confidence becomes more grounded, and your goals are pursued from a place of wholeness, not lack.

Let this be your reminder:
You do not need to be perfect to be worthy.
You do not need to fix yourself to be valuable.
You only need to come home to who you already are —
and choose to love her, fully and without condition.

Reflection Prompt:

What parts of yourself have you struggled to accept? What would it look like to offer those parts compassion instead of criticism?

Speak to Yourself with Kindness

The words we speak to ourselves shape the reality we live in.

Many of us have become fluent in self-criticism. We replay our mistakes, scrutinize our appearances, and judge our every move with a voice that is far harsher than we would ever use toward someone we love. Over time, this internal dialogue becomes so habitual that we rarely question it — and yet, its effects are deeply felt.

How we speak to ourselves matters.
Our inner voice becomes the narrator of our story, the architect of our self-image, and the filter through which we experience the world.

The Cost of Harsh Self-Talk

When we are constantly criticizing ourselves, we erode our confidence and sense of self-worth. We begin to internalize the belief that we are not good enough, smart enough, beautiful enough, or worthy enough. This creates a cycle of insecurity, anxiety, and emotional exhaustion — one that can sabotage our goals, our relationships, and our happiness.

What many fail to realize is that this inner harshness is not a form of self-improvement. It does not motivate or strengthen us. In fact, research shows that self-criticism activates the body's stress response, while self-compassion reduces stress and increases emotional resilience.

Simply put: kindness is not weakness. It is a source of strength.

Rewriting the Inner Script

Changing the way you speak to yourself begins with awareness. Pay attention to the tone and language of your inner voice. Would you speak to a friend the way you speak to yourself? Would you correct a child with such judgment or shame?

When you catch yourself using unkind or punishing language, pause. Take a breath. And choose again.

Speak to yourself with the same warmth, patience, and encouragement you would extend to someone you care about. Be gentle. Be honest, yes — but not cruel. There is a difference between accountability and abuse.

Your inner dialogue should be a safe space — a place where you are allowed to grow, stumble, rise, and begin again.

Words That Heal

Speaking to yourself with kindness does not mean ignoring your flaws or pretending everything is perfect. Rather, it means shifting from self-condemnation to self-support.

It is replacing:

- "I'm so stupid," with "I made a mistake, and I'm still learning."
- "I'm not good enough," with "I am enough, and I'm growing every day."
- "I failed," with "This experience taught me something valuable."

Kind self-talk is not about inflated positivity — it is about balanced truth. It acknowledges challenges, celebrates progress, and offers grace in the spaces in between.

Becoming Your Own Ally

When you consistently speak to yourself with kindness, you build trust within. You stop walking through life with a critic on your shoulder and start moving with a quiet, steady companion — one who believes in your worth even on the hard days.

You become your own ally. And from this place of inner peace and support, you begin to show up in the world with more confidence, more clarity, and more compassion — not just for yourself, but for others.

You Deserve a Loving Voice

Your inner voice is with you for life. Make it a loving one.

Let it remind you of your strength when you forget. Let it calm you when you're overwhelmed. Let it encourage you to take the next brave step forward. And above all, let it speak to you in a way that reflects how deeply worthy you are of tenderness, patience, and love.

Because you are.

Receive the Compliment — Learning to Welcome Love

One of the most telling signs of our relationship with ourselves is how we respond to a compliment.

For many, the moment someone offers kind words—whether it's about appearance, talent, intelligence, or kindness—the instinctive response is to deflect.
We downplay, dismiss, or shrink:
"Oh, this old thing?"
"It was nothing."
"Not really, but thank you."

While often said out of humility, these responses can be subtle forms of self-rejection. At their core, they reflect a discomfort with being seen, celebrated, and valued.

But learning to **accept a compliment** is not about arrogance. It's about alignment. It's about allowing the truth of your beauty, goodness, and worth to land—and stay.

Why We Struggle to Accept Compliments

There are many reasons why accepting a compliment can feel awkward or uncomfortable:

- **Low self-esteem** makes it hard to believe the kind words being said.
- **Perfectionism** tells us we don't deserve praise unless we've done everything flawlessly.
- **Cultural conditioning** may have taught us to be modest or self-deprecating, mistaking it for humility.
- **Fear of judgment** can make us afraid that acknowledging a compliment will come off as conceited.

But these are all rooted in the same limiting belief: *that we are not enough.*

When you reject a compliment, you are not only diminishing the positive moment—you are unconsciously reinforcing your own self-doubt. You are refusing to allow light in.

The Power of Receiving

Receiving is an act of openness. It requires vulnerability. It means allowing someone's positive perception of you to be true, even if a small part of you still doubts it.

But here is the truth: *Just because you are still learning to see your worth, doesn't mean it isn't there.*
Others may see your brilliance long before you do. And sometimes, their reflection becomes a mirror that helps you come home to yourself.

A compliment is not a debt to repay. It's a gift. And the most graceful response is simply, "Thank you."

Compliments as Mirrors

When someone tells you that you're talented, beautiful, inspiring, or kind—pause. Before brushing it off, take a breath and let their words settle in your heart.

Ask yourself: *What if that's true?*
What if the way they see you is real, and you've just been too close to notice?

Accepting compliments does not mean you believe you're better than others. It means you are finally willing to recognize the truth of your own light.

Practicing the Art of Receiving

Like any form of self-love, accepting compliments takes practice. Here are a few ways to cultivate the ability to receive:

Pause and breathe. Instead of rushing to respond, give yourself a second to receive the moment fully.

Smile and say thank you. This simple response acknowledges the kindness and affirms your worth without deflection.

Resist the urge to diminish. If someone compliments your outfit, resist saying, "It was on sale." If they praise your work, don't say, "It was just luck."

Let it affirm, not define. Compliments can affirm your value, but they are not your source of it. Let them land without becoming dependent on them.

Letting Love In

Accepting a compliment is a small but profound act of self-respect. It's a sign that you are beginning to believe in your own beauty, talent, and presence. More importantly, it is a sign that you are open to receiving love—not just from others, but from yourself.

You do not have to earn kindness. You do not have to justify your worth. You are allowed to be seen, celebrated, and cherished exactly as you are.

So the next time someone tells you, "You're amazing," don't argue.
Believe them.

Because maybe, just maybe… you are.

Affirmations to appreciate yourself today

I appreciate the person I am today.
I honor how far I've come.
I am proud of my growth, even the small steps.
I am grateful for my strengths and my softness.
I celebrate my uniqueness every day.
I am doing the best I can, and that is enough.
I give myself credit for showing up.
I value the lessons I've learned from my journey.
I see beauty in who I am becoming.
I am worthy of my own appreciation and love.

Chapter 2: The Roots of Low Self-Worth

Before we ever learn to think for ourselves, the world teaches us how to see ourselves.

From a young age, we are shaped by forces outside of our control — by family beliefs, school systems, cultural norms, media images, and societal expectations. These early influences form the foundation of our identity and sense of worth. They tell us who we're supposed to be, what success looks like, how love is earned, and which parts of ourselves are acceptable — or not.

This is what we call **childhood conditioning** and **societal programming**. And for many of us, it becomes the invisible script we carry into adulthood, often unaware that it's running our lives.

But here is the truth:
If we are to truly love ourselves — fully, freely, and unapologetically — we must first unlearn what never belonged to us.

The Roots of Conditioning

Childhood conditioning begins with messages we receive early in life, especially from caregivers and authority figures. These messages may have been direct or subtle, spoken or implied:

- "Be a good girl and don't make a scene."
- "You're too sensitive."
- "Success means getting straight A's."
- "Love is earned when you behave perfectly."
- "Your worth depends on how others see you."

Even when well-intentioned, these beliefs can plant seeds of insecurity, fear, and self-rejection. We internalize them and adapt to survive — often by dimming our light, silencing our needs, or striving endlessly to please.

Societal programming then reinforces these beliefs on a larger scale. We are bombarded with media that defines beauty narrowly, glorifies busyness over balance, and teaches us that value is tied to productivity, wealth, or appearance. We're encouraged to chase perfection rather than authenticity — comparison over connection.

By the time we reach adulthood, many of us are no longer living *as ourselves* — we are living as who we were *taught* to be.

The Impact of Unquestioned Beliefs

When you carry beliefs you never chose, you build a life that doesn't reflect who you truly are. You may find yourself:

- Achieving goals that don't fulfill you
- Dismissing your emotions to appear "strong"
- Staying silent to avoid conflict
- Seeking external approval for every decision
- Feeling guilty for resting, dreaming, or choosing differently

This disconnection from self creates inner tension. Deep down, your soul knows there's more to you. More depth, more truth, more freedom. But as long as you're living by someone else's definition of "enough," that truth remains hidden under layers of conditioning.

The Courage to Unlearn

Self-love is not just about affirming your worth — it's about **reclaiming it** from the systems and stories that distorted it.

This begins with **awareness**. Start to notice the beliefs you've been living by and ask:

- *Where did this come from?*
- *Is this actually true for me?*
- *Does this belief bring me closer to myself, or further away?*

Next comes **permission** — the radical permission to choose new thoughts, new values, and new ways of being. You are allowed to redefine what success means. You are allowed to honor your emotions. You are allowed to show up as your full, imperfect self — even if it challenges what you were taught.

Unlearning is not rebellion for the sake of it — it's liberation. It's returning to your most authentic self, the one who existed before the world told you who to be.

Returning Home to You

As you dismantle these inherited beliefs, you make space for self-trust. You stop living life to meet external expectations and begin living in alignment with your inner truth.

You'll notice:

- Your decisions come from intuition, not fear.

- Your self-worth no longer rises and falls with opinions or outcomes.
- You begin to define happiness, success, beauty, and love *on your own terms*.
- You live from a place of empowerment, not programming.

This is the real work of self-love. Not just loving the parts of you that were praised — but learning to love the parts of you that were once rejected, repressed, or misunderstood.

You Are the Author Now

You were handed a script. But you do not have to keep reading it.

You have the power to revise, rewrite, and redefine who you are and how you live. Every time you question a limiting belief, you break a generational pattern. Every time you honor your truth over expectation, you heal.

This chapter is your invitation to choose a new narrative. Not the one given to you — the one that belongs to you.

You are no longer bound by who they told you to be. You are free to become who you truly are.

How Trauma, Comparison, and Toxic Relationships Undermine Self-Love

Self-love does not exist in a vacuum. It is shaped, nurtured, or wounded by our life experiences—especially the painful ones.

Behind every person struggling to love themselves is often a trail of hidden pain: a moment when they were told they weren't enough, a relationship that chipped away at their confidence, or a silent comparison that made them question their value. These wounds don't always scream—they whisper. They disguise themselves as self-doubt, people-pleasing, perfectionism, or emotional numbness. And unless we confront them, they quietly govern our sense of worth.

The Lingering Echo of Trauma

Trauma—whether emotional, physical, or psychological—is not always about what happened, but what it caused you to believe about yourself.

Maybe it was childhood neglect, where love felt conditional.
Maybe it was abuse that blurred your sense of safety and trust.
Maybe it was loss, rejection, or betrayal that made you feel unworthy of being chosen.

These experiences, especially if left unprocessed, plant deep-rooted beliefs like:

- "I am not lovable."
- "I must prove my worth."
- "If I show my true self, I'll be hurt or abandoned."

Trauma creates emotional armor. You begin to build walls to protect yourself—but sometimes, those same walls keep love out, even self-love. You learn to survive, not thrive. And in that survival, your authentic self begins to fade.

But here's the truth: **You are not what happened to you.**
Your past may have shaped your story, but it does not define your value.
Healing does not erase the pain—it rewrites the meaning. And it starts with validating your experience, speaking your truth, and giving yourself the safety you never had.

Trust Yourself

Trusting yourself is one of the most radical acts of self-love. It means believing that your inner voice is worth listening to — even when it contradicts the noise around you. It means recognizing that deep within you lies wisdom shaped by your experiences, intuition, and soul — not something to be second-guessed, but honored.

But here's the truth: You know more than you think you do. Your instincts are not random; they are signals. That uneasy feeling in your stomach? That spark of inspiration that won't go away? Those quiet whispers urging you forward or warning you to turn back — that's *you* communicating with you.

Trusting yourself is a skill. It requires practice, patience, and courage. Start by listening — really listening — to what your body, heart, and intuition are trying to say. Reflect on the times in your past when you knew something without evidence, or made a decision that felt right even if it didn't make sense to anyone else. That was inner trust. And it was never wrong.

Stop outsourcing your power. You don't need everyone to agree with your choices to know they're right for you. You don't need to explain or justify your truth. You just need to own it.

Avoiding Comparison

Comparison is the thief of joy—but more than that, it is the assassin of self-worth.

In the digital age, where perfectly curated lives are on display 24/7, it is easy to feel like you are not doing enough, achieving enough, or even *being* enough. You may find yourself scrolling through highlight reels, unconsciously measuring your beauty, success, or happiness against someone else's filtered image.

But comparison is fundamentally flawed. You are comparing your *behind-the-scenes* with someone else's *final cut*. You are measuring your internal journey with someone else's external projection.

The result? You diminish your uniqueness. You mute your magic. You begin to see yourself as lacking, even when you are whole.

Self-love means learning to **honor your own timeline**, your own rhythm, your own voice. Your worth is not relative—it is inherent. You are incomparable, because you were never meant to be a copy of anyone else.

Toxic Relationships and the Loss of Identity

Some of the deepest wounds are not inflicted by enemies, but by the people we once trusted most—partners, family, friends.

Toxic relationships are marked by control, manipulation, emotional abuse, and subtle forms of invalidation. Over time, they can cause you to question your judgment, suppress your needs, and sacrifice your identity for the sake of peace.

You begin to internalize the lies:

- "I'm too emotional."
- "I deserve this treatment."
- "If I were better, they'd treat me better."

This erosion of self happens gradually, often without realizing it. You shrink. You overextend. You accept less than you deserve—and call it love.

But healthy love does not require you to abandon yourself. It does not silence your truth or dim your light. Real love reinforces self-love. It feels safe, respectful, and reciprocal.

Leaving a toxic relationship—whether romantic, familial, or platonic—takes immense courage. But it is also a profound act of self-respect. You are not selfish for choosing peace. You are not difficult for demanding respect. You are not unlovable because someone failed to love you well.

Recognizing the Limiting Beliefs Holding You Back

We are not born doubting ourselves.

As children, we dream boldly. We ask for what we want. We speak our minds without shame. But somewhere along the way, we begin to absorb beliefs that tell us who we *should* be, what we *can't* do, and why we are *not enough*.

These beliefs often take root quietly — passed down by parents, teachers, peers, or society. They become so ingrained in our identity that we rarely question them. They dictate our choices, silence our voice, and sabotage our potential — all while operating in the background of our minds like invisible chains.

These are called **limiting beliefs**, and they are often the greatest barrier to self-love and personal freedom.

What Are Limiting Beliefs?

Limiting beliefs are subconscious thoughts or assumptions we accept as truth that restrict us in some way. They often begin with phrases like:

- "I'm not good enough."
- "I don't deserve love."
- "Success is for other people."
- "If I try, I'll fail."
- "I'm too old / too young / too broken."

These beliefs are not objective facts — they are *stories* we've internalized. And the most dangerous part? We act as if they are true. We unconsciously make decisions, form relationships, and set goals based on these silent scripts, never realizing how much they hold us back.

Where Do They Come From?

Limiting beliefs are often rooted in:

- **Childhood experiences**: Being constantly criticized, ignored, or compared can lead to beliefs like "I'm not worthy" or "I must earn love."

- **Cultural or societal norms**: Messages about gender, race, appearance, or success can condition us to feel "less than" or "not enough."
- **Past failures or trauma**: Painful events can reinforce beliefs that we are incapable, unworthy, or cursed to repeat the past.
- **Toxic relationships**: Constant belittling, gaslighting, or emotional abuse can distort our self-perception and confidence.

The origin may vary, but the effect is the same: we build walls where we once had wings.

How to Recognize Your Limiting Beliefs

Awareness is the first step toward change. Begin by noticing your inner dialogue, especially in moments of stress, fear, or self-doubt. Ask yourself:

- What do I tell myself when I fail or get rejected?
- What fears stop me from taking risks?
- In what areas of life do I feel stuck or unworthy?
- What do I believe I *can't* have — and why?

Often, these beliefs show up through patterns: repeated self-sabotage, staying small, avoiding opportunities, or staying in unhealthy environments.

Once you identify a limiting belief, gently question it:

- *Is this belief absolutely true?*
- *Where did it come from?*
- *What evidence do I have that contradicts it?*
- *Who might I be without this belief?*

You'll likely find that these beliefs were inherited — not chosen.

Replacing Limiting Beliefs with Empowering Truths

The beautiful truth is that beliefs can be rewritten. You do not have to remain loyal to thoughts that belittle your potential.

Begin replacing limiting beliefs with **empowering affirmations** that align with your truth:

- "I am more than enough just as I am."
- "I am worthy of love and success."
- "I trust myself to grow through every challenge."
- "My past does not define my future."
- "I am free to become all that I desire."

This work is not about blind positivity. It's about choosing beliefs that uplift, guide, and reflect your highest self.

It takes time. Repetition. Patience. But with each new truth, you loosen the grip of old programming. You return to your power — the power to choose how you see yourself and what you believe you're capable of.

The Freedom of Conscious Belief

When you dismantle the limiting beliefs you've carried, something remarkable happens:
You expand. You begin to take up more space in your own life. You dream bigger, love deeper, and speak louder — not from a place of ego, but from a place of worthiness.

You stop settling and start thriving. You stop performing and start living.

And most of all, you finally begin to love yourself — not for who you were told to be, but for who you truly are.

You are not your past.
You are not your fear.
You are not your limiting beliefs.

You are infinite possibility — waiting to be claimed.

Reflection Prompt:

What is one limiting belief you've accepted as truth? Write it down. Then write a new, empowering belief to replace it. Speak it aloud. Repeat it daily. Choose it intentionally.

Affirmations to increase self- love and self-respect

I deserve love and respect.
I am kind to myself.
I am enough just as I am.
I treat myself with care.
I listen to my needs.
I don't need to be perfect to be worthy.
I believe in myself.
I choose peace and protect my energy.
I trust myself more each day.
I love who I am becoming.

Chapter 3 Love and Respect Yourself

Value Your Life — The Privilege of Being Here

Sometimes, we forget just how miraculous it is to wake up.

Not because we are ungrateful, but because we're busy—rushing, surviving, fixing, proving. Life becomes something to get through instead of something to *cherish*. But when we slow down, breathe, and truly become present, we start to realize the astonishing truth:

Being alive—right now, in this exact moment—is a privilege.

The Gift You Didn't Ask For—but Were Chosen To Receive

Think about it. Of all the infinite possibilities, *you* were given this life.

You didn't have to earn the air you breathe. You didn't have to apply for the rhythm of your heart. And yet, you were entrusted with this body, this mind, this story. You were given the ability to think, to love, to cry, to start over. You were placed here, at this exact time in history, to experience life fully.

That alone is extraordinary.

But when we're caught in pain, failure, comparison, or routine, we can forget that life isn't just about obligations or goals—it's also about *wonder*. And the more you begin to love yourself, the more you awaken to the truth that your very existence is worthy of reverence.

You Are Not an Accident

Life is not random. And you are not a mistake.

Your presence here means that you are part of something much greater than yourself. Whether you believe in divine timing, spiritual design, or simply the beauty of nature—you were chosen to *be*.

That means your life has value beyond productivity or perfection.
You don't have to be someone else to be significant.

You don't have to do more to matter.
You are already enough by simply existing.

And isn't that freeing?

Reclaiming the Beauty of the Ordinary

To value your life doesn't mean every day is a celebration or a grand breakthrough. It means learning to honor the small, overlooked things—the sound of laughter, the way your dog greets you, the smell of your favorite candle, the quiet peace of your own company.

These are not meaningless details. They are *life*.

Too often we think, "When I finally succeed, then I'll be grateful." But gratitude is not a reward—it's a *practice*. And when you begin to see your life as sacred, everything softens. You begin to feel worthy, not just of success or love, but of *being here*.

The Power of Presence

When you begin to value your life, you stop rushing through it.
You start noticing the way the sun filters through your window.
You savor your morning coffee instead of gulping it down.

You become aware of your breath—and you thank your body for carrying you through another day.

Loving yourself means realizing that your life doesn't need to be perfect to be precious.

It already is.

Choosing to Stay, Choosing to Shine

There may be times when life feels heavy. When you question your path, your worth, your place in this world. But even in those moments, there is something unbreakable inside you—the will to keep going, the quiet whisper that says, *I'm still here.*

That whisper is sacred. It means you haven't given up. It means you still have hope. It means there is more for you—more healing, more joy, more love.

And that, in itself, is proof that your life is *valuable.*

The Power of Positive Self-Talk

There's a voice you hear every day—more than any friend, mentor, or loved one.

It's the voice inside your head.
The one that narrates your thoughts, questions your decisions, and sometimes whispers doubts when you need courage the most.

This voice is your self-talk. And whether you realize it or not, it's shaping the quality of your life.

Words Become Beliefs

If someone followed you around all day and constantly criticized you, would you feel confident? Probably not.

Yet many of us do this to ourselves every single day.

We call ourselves names we'd never dare say to a friend: *You're so stupid. You'll never succeed. You're not good enough.* And then we wonder why our self-esteem is fragile, why we doubt our dreams, or why we settle for less than we deserve.

But here's the good news: *You can change the way you speak to yourself—starting today.*

Because positive self-talk isn't about being delusional.
It's about being intentional.
It's not pretending life is perfect. It's reminding yourself that *you are capable, resilient, and worthy* even when things go wrong.

How I Changed My Inner Dialogue

I didn't always speak kindly to myself. For years, my mind was a battlefield. Any mistake turned into a personal attack. I was my own harshest critic—thinking if I was hard enough on myself, I'd somehow become better.

But I didn't become better. I became exhausted. Anxious. Small.

It wasn't until I read a simple quote that everything changed:

"You talk to yourself more than anyone else. Be careful what you say."

It stopped me in my tracks. I realized that the one relationship I could never escape—the one with *me*—was being poisoned by negativity.

So I made a quiet promise: *I will speak to myself like someone I love.*

I started small. A compliment here, a word of encouragement there. I wrote sticky notes on my mirror with phrases like:

- "You're doing your best, and that's enough."
- "You are worthy of rest."
- "You don't need to be perfect to be powerful."

It felt awkward at first. But with time, those words became my truth. I started showing up differently. More open. More confident. More *me*.

Rewriting the Script

Think of your self-talk as the script to your life. The more you repeat something, the more it becomes your reality.

Here's how you begin shifting that script:

Catch the Critic: Awareness is key. Notice when your inner dialogue turns negative.

Pause and Reframe: Ask, *Would I say this to someone I love?* If not, change the language.

Use Affirmations with Feeling: Speak words of strength and say them *like you mean them*. Your tone matters.

Celebrate Progress, Not Perfection: Instead of focusing on what's missing, acknowledge how far you've come.

Over time, these small shifts create powerful change. Your inner voice becomes your ally—not your enemy.

Speak Love Into Your Life

You don't have to wait to be more successful, more attractive, or more accomplished to start being kind to yourself.

Speak love into your mornings.
Speak forgiveness into your mistakes.
Speak confidence into your challenges.
Speak grace into your healing.

When your self-talk is rooted in compassion, your whole life begins to reflect it. You start attracting people and opportunities that match the way you see yourself—whole, radiant, and deeply deserving.

Reflection Prompt:

What is one negative phrase you frequently say to yourself? Rewrite it into a positive, empowering affirmation. Repeat it daily for the next seven days.

Know Your Worth

There comes a moment in every woman's life when she wakes up and realizes—*she's been underestimating herself.*

Not just in relationships.
Not just at work.
But in the quiet places of her own soul.

She's been settling for less than she deserves, not because she's weak, but because somewhere along the way, she forgot her value. She forgot how deeply worthy she's always been.

This chapter is about *remembering.*

You Were Born Worthy

Worth is not something you earn.
It's something you *are.*

From the moment you took your first breath, you were valuable. Not because of what you could do, produce, or prove—but simply because you exist.

You don't have to reach a goal, fit into a dress size, or be in a relationship to have worth. Your value is not conditional. It is *inherent.* It cannot be taken from you, though the world may try to convince you otherwise.

Knowing your worth means you stop waiting for permission to feel enough. You stop shrinking, explaining, or apologizing for your presence.

You stand tall in the truth that:
You are enough. Right now. As you are.

How I Forgot—And Then Reclaimed My Worth

There was a time when I tied my worth to everything outside of myself.

If someone loved me, I felt lovable.
If I got the job, I felt smart.
If I looked good, I felt beautiful.
But the moment those things faded—even briefly—so did my self-worth.

One day, after yet another disappointment in love, I looked in the mirror and asked, "Why do I keep settling for less than I deserve?"

And the answer was clear: *Because I didn't believe I deserved more.*

That was my turning point. I stopped chasing validation and started building a relationship with the one person I had abandoned—*myself.* I began investing in my growth, setting boundaries, and walking away from anything that made me question my value.

It wasn't always easy, but with every small step, I reclaimed the power I had unknowingly given away.

Signs You've Forgotten Your Worth

Sometimes we don't realize we've lost sight of our value until the symptoms become too loud to ignore:

- Saying "yes" when you mean "no"
- Accepting disrespect and calling it love
- Undercharging for your work or overworking to feel "useful"
- Comparing yourself to others constantly
- Doubting your abilities even when you're qualified
- Staying silent to keep the peace

If any of this feels familiar, don't judge yourself. *Forgive yourself.* And then choose differently. Because knowing your worth is not about arrogance—it's about alignment.

What Happens When You Know Your Worth

When you know your worth:

- You stop chasing people who make you feel hard to love.
- You speak up, not to be liked, but because your voice matters.
- You make decisions from a place of *power*, not fear.
- You stop settling—and start *selecting*.
- You attract opportunities, relationships, and experiences that match your elevated self-belief.

And most importantly, you learn to walk away from anything that doesn't honor the light within you.

You Are the Standard

When you know your worth, you become the standard. You no longer try to fit into someone else's mold—you *set the mold*.
You no longer ask, "Am I good enough for them?"
Instead, you ask, *"Are they good enough for me?"*

This is not ego. This is self-respect.

This is what happens when a woman finally chooses herself.

How to Release the Fear of Judgment

Letting go of the need for validation is a process, but it begins with awareness and small acts of courage:

Understand Projection
People's opinions often say more about them than about you. Their fears, insecurities, and limitations are not yours to carry.

Affirm Your Self-Worth
Repeat daily: *I am not here to please everyone. I am here to be fully myself.*

Take Small Risks
Speak your truth, share your ideas, or make bold choices—even if it feels uncomfortable. Growth lies on the other side of discomfort.

Surround Yourself with Authenticity
Spend time with people who celebrate your realness—not those who expect a version of you that fits their mold.

How to Build Unshakable Self-Esteem

Self-esteem is the silent force that shapes how you show up in the world.

It determines what you tolerate, what you believe you're capable of, and what you allow yourself to receive.

When your self-esteem is high, you trust yourself, speak kindly to yourself, and walk through life with a quiet yet undeniable confidence. But when it's low, everything feels harder: relationships, career, self-expression, even the simple act of believing you deserve happiness.

The good news is this: **Self-esteem isn't fixed. It can be nurtured, healed, and elevated.**
And it starts with how you choose to treat yourself—right now.

What Is Self-Esteem, Really?

Self-esteem is your internal estimate of your worthiness and value. It's the way you regard yourself in your own heart and mind.

It's not ego. It's not arrogance.
It's the deep, unwavering belief that:

"I matter. I am capable. I am worthy of good things."

Many of us develop fractured self-esteem through childhood wounds, repeated rejection, criticism, or comparison. But you are not defined by where you've been—you are empowered by where you choose to go.

My Own Path to Rebuilding Confidence

I didn't always feel confident. In fact, for years, I looked strong on the outside—but internally, I was quietly battling self-doubt. I questioned everything I did, second-guessed my abilities, and let others' opinions define me.

But one day, I decided to stop waiting for someone else to validate me.
Instead, I became my own source of approval.

I started speaking to myself with kindness.
I acknowledged my small wins.
I stopped apologizing for taking up space.
And slowly but surely, I began to feel different. Stronger. More whole.

Confidence didn't arrive overnight. But self-respect did. And that changed everything.

Tips to Increase Your Self-Esteem

Here are practices and mindset shifts that truly work—no fluff, just real transformation:

Keep Promises to Yourself

Every time you say you'll do something and follow through, your self-esteem rises. Whether it's waking up early, working out, or setting a boundary, these acts build *self-trust*. Confidence blooms from consistency.

"I do what I say I will do—even for myself."

Celebrate Small Wins

Don't wait for massive achievements to feel proud. Start noticing the little victories—getting out of bed on a hard day, speaking your truth, staying calm when you wanted to lash out. These moments are gold.

Write them down. Speak them aloud. Let yourself feel proud.

Speak to Yourself Like Someone You Love

Your inner voice becomes your reality. Replace self-criticism with compassion.
Say things like:

- *"I'm learning, and that's okay."*
- *"I handled that better than before."*
- *"I am worthy of love, even when I'm imperfect."*

Kindness rewires your self-perception.

Surround Yourself with Supportive Energy

You become like the people you spend time with.
Choose friends, mentors, and environments that uplift, encourage, and believe in your potential. If you can't find them yet, be that person for yourself.

Stop Comparing, Start Honoring

Comparison is the thief of joy—and the destroyer of self-esteem.
Instead of asking, "Why am I not like them?"
Ask, *"What makes me special?"*

You are not here to duplicate anyone. You are here to fully become *you*.

Take Aligned Action

Confidence isn't built in thought—it's built in motion.
Start the project. Say the thing. Take the risk.
You don't need to feel 100% ready—just willing to try.
Action breeds confidence. Always.

Your Value Is Not Up for Debate

You are not defined by your past.
You are not limited by your mistakes.
You are not less than anyone else.

Your value is not determined by numbers, followers, partners, or opinions. It is *yours*, sacred and whole.

The more you act like you matter, the more you'll begin to *feel* like you matter.

And once you do, the world will begin to reflect it back to you.

Chapter 4 Live Intentionally

A Story of Choosing Purpose Over Passivity

I used to wake up and grab my phone before I even opened both eyes.
Emails. Notifications. A flood of other people's thoughts, opinions, and expectations would pour in before I'd even asked myself how I felt. The day would start *for* me, not *with* me.

And so I spent years living on autopilot.
Reacting, rushing, pleasing, posting.
Checking boxes, but never really checking in with my soul.

One night, I sat alone in my apartment, lights off, phone buzzing somewhere across the room. I felt hollow. Like I had been everywhere for everyone—but nowhere for myself.

That was the night I whispered a question that would change everything:

"What would it look like if I started living *on purpose?*"

The Shift: From Default to Design

Living intentionally means *you choose* how your life unfolds.
It means you pause before reacting. You say yes only when your soul says yes too.
It's no longer about rushing to meet other people's timelines—but about honoring your own rhythm.

So I started small.

Each morning, I gave myself five minutes of silence. No phone. No noise. Just breath and presence.

I asked:

- What do *I* need today?
- What energy do I want to bring into this day?
- What can I let go of that isn't aligned?

From there, my entire life started to shift—not suddenly, but steadily.

I stopped overcommitting.
I started nourishing my body because I *loved* it, not because I hated it.
I surrounded myself with beauty and simplicity.
I turned off the noise to hear my own voice again.

The Power of Intention in Everyday Life

Living intentionally is not about having a perfect plan—it's about being *present and conscious* in your choices.

Ask yourself:

- Why am I doing this?
- Does it align with the life I want to create?
- Am I acting from love or fear?

Even your smallest habits—how you wake up, how you speak to yourself, how you spend your evenings—shape the person you are becoming.

So why not design a life you are proud to call yours?

Let Your Heart Be the Compass

The world will try to pull you in a thousand directions. But intention is your anchor. It brings you back to what *matters*.

When you live intentionally:

- You create boundaries instead of burning out.
- You listen to your intuition rather than noise.
- You give your time and energy to people and projects that nurture you.

You stop chasing the life that impresses others—and start building the one that fulfills *you*.

Know What Matters — Identifying Your Core Values

There was a moment in my life when everything looked *fine* from the outside—successful job, supportive friends, daily routine that "should" have made me feel grateful. And yet, I felt a quiet ache in my chest.

Something was missing.

I wasn't unhappy. But I wasn't fully alive either.
I had achieved what others said I *should* want—but none of it truly reflected *me*.

That's when I learned something powerful:

You can build a beautiful life, and still feel lost—if it isn't rooted in your values.

What Are Core Values?

Core values are the fundamental truths you hold about what truly matters in life.
They are not goals, roles, or achievements.
They are your internal compass—guiding how you live, love, decide, and show up.

When you live in alignment with your values, life feels richer, more peaceful, more *true*.
When you don't, you feel disconnected, anxious, or stuck—even if everything looks "good" on paper.

The Day I Realized I Was Living Against My Own Values

I remember being invited to a high-profile event—fancy venue, powerful people, a place where "success" would be measured by visibility. I said yes, but the moment I arrived, I felt hollow. I wasn't interested in networking or impressing. I longed for real conversations, quiet presence, deep connection.

I realized that *authenticity* and *meaningful connection* were values of mine—and this world I had been chasing wasn't honoring them.

That was a turning point. I began reevaluating everything.

Why Values Matter for Self-Love

Knowing your values gives you clarity.
It helps you make aligned decisions, set boundaries without guilt, and stop seeking external validation.

Self-love isn't just bubble baths and journaling. It's having the courage to say:

"This is what matters to me. This is who I am. This is how I choose to live."

When you act in alignment with your values, you stop betraying yourself.
And that's where deep self-respect begins.

How to Discover Your Core Values

Here's a gentle, powerful exercise to uncover your values:

1. Reflect on Peak Moments

Think about three times in your life when you felt most alive, proud, or fulfilled.
Ask yourself:

- What was happening?

- Who were you with?
- What made that moment meaningful?

You'll likely find clues—freedom, creativity, connection, purpose.

2. Identify Anger or Frustration

What kinds of situations deeply irritate or exhaust you? Often, they violate a core value.
For example, if dishonesty infuriates you, *integrity* may be a core value.

3. List and Choose

Make a list of 20 words that resonate with you. Then narrow it down to your top 5.
Some examples:

- Freedom
- Growth
- Authenticity
- Joy
- Kindness

- Peace
- Justice
- Simplicity
- Courage
- Love

These are your anchors. Your truth.

4. Ask: Am I Living in Alignment?

Look at your current choices, relationships, and career.
Are they aligned with your top values?
If not—where can you make subtle shifts to come home to yourself?

Living Your Values Is an Act of Self-Love

Once you know your values, protect them.

Let them guide your decisions.
Let them shape your goals.
Let them help you say no with confidence and yes with heart.

Living in alignment with your core values won't always be easy—but it will always be *right* for your soul.

Make a Pie Chart of Your Life

Seeing Your Life with Clarity and Compassion

I once sat in a quiet room, journaling after a particularly emotional week. I had felt scattered, exhausted, disconnected—from my goals, from myself, from my joy.

That's when I asked myself a powerful question: **"Where is all my energy going?"**

So, I drew a circle.
I sliced it into pieces based on how I had spent my time and thoughts that week—work, scrolling, worrying about others' opinions, helping friends, trying to please, resting, dreaming, loving, learning.

And when I stepped back and looked at that little hand-drawn pie chart, I felt a wave of truth rush over me.

I had given so much to everything and everyone— except myself.

That circle became a mirror. And from it, I began to realign my life.

What a Pie Chart Can Reveal

When you draw a pie chart of your life, you're not just creating a visual.
You're holding up a magnifying glass to your reality. It reveals:

- Where your energy is flowing
- What takes priority (intentionally or by default)
- Whether your actions align with your values
- Why you may feel fulfilled—or drained

The beauty is, the pie chart doesn't lie.

How to Make Your Life Pie Chart

Here's how to create this eye-opening reflection:

Step 1: Draw a Circle

This circle represents 100% of your energy, time, and attention in a typical week.

Step 2: Slice the Circle

Divide the circle into segments based on where your energy goes.
Some categories to consider:

- Work
- Family
- Relationships
- Social media
- Physical health
- Mental health
- Creative expression
- Personal growth
- Rest & solitude
- Worrying or overthinking
- Helping others
- Spirituality

Be honest—this isn't about judgment. It's about awareness.

Step 3: Label & Reflect

Once your pie chart is labeled, ask yourself:

- *Is this how I want to live my life?*
- *What feels overfed? What's starved?*
- *Which areas energize me? Which drain me?*
- *How much time am I actually giving to loving, caring for, and growing myself?*

The Power of Awareness

This visual can be jarring. You might discover that:

- You spend more time worrying than creating
- Your phone gets more attention than your dreams
- You give more to others than you give yourself

And yet, that's the gift.
Because once you see the imbalance, **you can shift it**.

Redesign Your Life Pie

Here's the empowering part:
Draw a second pie chart—this time showing how you *want* to live.

What would a life that reflects self-love, peace, and purpose look like?

- Maybe less overthinking, more meditation
- Fewer toxic conversations, more nourishing relationships
- Less people-pleasing, more boundaries
- Less numbing, more dreaming

The space you give to each piece of your life speaks volumes about how you value yourself.

From Auto-Pilot to Intention

Too many of us live by default.
But your energy is your most sacred currency. Where you spend it shapes your life.

So ask yourself:

Am I spending my life or investing it?

Living with intention means taking back the pen—and redrawing the circle in a way that feels honest and empowering.

Growing Into Wholeness

Finding Growth Psychologically, Spiritually, and Physically

There comes a time in your life when you no longer crave just surface-level success.
You want something deeper.
You want to feel whole.

True self-love isn't limited to one area of your life.
It's a multi-dimensional journey—one that nourishes your mind, your soul, and your body.
It's about becoming the *fullest expression of yourself*—not just what the world sees, but what you carry within.

This chapter is your invitation to step into that fuller version of you by growing from the inside out.

Psychological Growth: Rewiring the Mind

Your thoughts create the lens through which you experience the world.
If that lens is dirty with self-doubt, fear, or unresolved trauma, it distorts everything—even love.

Psychological growth is the work of tending to your inner world. It requires:

- **Awareness** – Noticing your limiting beliefs, recurring thoughts, and emotional triggers.
- **Healing** – Acknowledging wounds from your past and seeking support when needed (therapy, journaling, inner child work).
- **Resilience** – Learning how to self-regulate, set boundaries, and stay rooted in your truth.

When you grow psychologically, you become emotionally intelligent, mentally strong, and *deeply self-aware*. You no longer operate on autopilot. You respond with clarity instead of reacting from old patterns.

This is the mind's liberation—and it is a form of self-love that lasts a lifetime.

Spiritual Growth: Reconnecting with the Soul

Spiritual growth isn't about religion. It's about *relationship*—with yourself, with life, and with something greater.

It's about trusting the process, surrendering control, and listening to the whisper within that says, *You are not alone. You are guided.*

Spiritual growth involves:

- **Silence** – Making space for stillness through meditation, prayer, or mindful walks.
- **Surrender** – Letting go of the need to control outcomes and embracing trust.
- **Meaning** – Asking deeper questions: Why am I here? What matters most? What is my soul's truth?

When you grow spiritually, you begin to feel a deeper peace—one that doesn't come from accomplishments, but from connection. You realize you are supported by life itself, and that even your hardest moments hold sacred purpose.

That kind of growth roots you, grounds you, and fills the empty spaces success alone cannot touch.

Physical Growth: Honoring the Body

Your body is not just a vessel—it's a sacred home.
It carries your spirit, your energy, your ability to move through life. It deserves reverence, not punishment.

Physical growth is about developing a new relationship with your body—one based on love, not shame.

This includes:

- **Movement** – Finding ways to move that bring joy, not guilt. Dance, yoga, walking, strength training—whatever makes you feel *alive*.
- **Nutrition** – Nourishing your body from a place of respect, not restriction.
- **Rest** – Understanding that rest is productive. Rest is healing. Rest is self-love.

When you grow physically, you begin to trust your body again. You stop treating it like an enemy and start seeing it as an ally in your growth.

Why All Three Matter

Growth is holistic. You cannot flourish by focusing on just one part of you.

- A sharp mind without peace is anxiety.
- A spiritual connection without self-awareness is imbalance.
- A strong body without inner healing is a façade.

When you grow psychologically, spiritually, and physically—you come *into alignment*.
You feel at home in your mind. At peace in your soul. Empowered in your body.

That's when you become magnetic. Grounded. Whole.

Realize There Will Never Be a Perfect Time to Prioritize What You Want

One of the biggest obstacles to growth—and to self-love—is waiting for the "perfect moment" to begin. We tell ourselves:

"I'll start when things settle down."
"Once I have more time, I'll focus on myself."
"After this project, then I can put my needs first."

But here's a truth many of us resist: **That perfect time does not exist.**

Life is messy. It is unpredictable. Responsibilities will always show up. Challenges will arise. Waiting for everything to line up perfectly means putting your own happiness and growth perpetually on hold.

If you wait for ideal conditions, you may never start.

Why We Wait

Waiting often comes from fear:

- Fear of judgment for putting yourself first
- Fear of failure or not doing things "right"
- Fear of adding "one more thing" to a busy schedule

Sometimes, it's just habit—believing that self-care and personal goals are luxuries, not necessities.

What Happens When You Wait

When you delay prioritizing what you want, you lose precious time.

You risk burnout, resentment, and disconnecting from your true self.
You teach yourself that your desires don't matter as much as others' demands.

How to Break the Cycle

Start small. Start now.

Prioritizing yourself doesn't have to mean overhauling your life overnight. It can be a five-minute meditation, saying "no" to one extra task, or writing down one personal goal.

Shift your mindset:
Your growth and happiness are not extras—they are essentials. When you care for yourself, you show up stronger for others.

Embrace imperfection:
There will always be distractions and unfinished tasks. That's life.
Choosing yourself in the midst of chaos is an act of courage—and the truest form of self-love.

A Personal Note

I once waited years for the "right time" to pursue my dreams—only to realize that time was now, imperfect as it was. When I finally said, "Enough waiting," my life changed.

The secret is this:
Your time is now.
Not perfect, not flawless, but real—and that is more than enough.

Reflection Prompt:

What's one small step you can take today to prioritize yourself—right now, imperfect as the moment may be?

Getting Organized with Your Time and Money

Self-love thrives when you respect and manage two of your most valuable resources: **time** and **money**. How you organize these directly impacts your ability to prioritize yourself, pursue your goals, and live intentionally.

Why Time and Money Matter

Both time and money are finite. You can never get them back once they're spent. Treating them thoughtfully is a powerful act of self-respect.

When you organize your time well, you create space for what matters most—whether that's growth, rest, creativity, or connection.
When you organize your money wisely, you reduce stress and gain freedom to invest in your happiness and future.

Organizing Your Time

Track Where Your Time Goes
Start by paying attention to how you spend your hours each day. Use a journal or an app to log your activities for a few days.
This awareness helps you identify time-wasters and pockets where you can reclaim minutes.

Prioritize Your Priorities
Make a list of your top priorities—both big and small. Then schedule them into your day like important appointments. Protect these times fiercely.

Set Boundaries
Learn to say "no" or "not now" to requests that drain your energy or distract you from your goals. Boundaries free up time and preserve your focus.

Use Tools and Rituals
Calendars, planners, timers, and daily routines can help structure your day and build momentum. Find what works for you and stick with it.

Organizing Your Money

Know Your Income and Expenses
Create a simple budget that tracks all sources of income and monthly expenses. This doesn't have to be complicated—just clear.

Set Financial Goals
Whether it's saving for a course, investing in your wellness, or paying off debt, specific goals motivate disciplined spending.

Automate Savings
Set up automatic transfers to a savings or emergency fund. Paying yourself first is a self-love habit that builds security.

Spend Mindfully
Before making purchases, ask:
Does this align with my values?
Does this support my growth or happiness?
Mindful spending turns money management into a meaningful practice, not a source of stress.

The Connection Between Time and Money

Time and money often influence each other. For example:

- Organizing your finances well can save you time worrying and scrambling.
- Managing your time efficiently can lead to better financial decisions and opportunities.

When you master both, you create a foundation that supports your self-love, goals, and peace of mind.

Establish a Daily Routine

A daily routine is more than just a checklist—it is a powerful framework that anchors your day and nurtures your well-being.
When you create a routine aligned with your values and

goals, you reduce overwhelm, boost productivity, and invite calm into your life.

Why a Routine Matters

Life can feel chaotic when you're constantly reacting to what comes at you. A routine gives you structure and predictability, which:

- Conserves mental energy by reducing decisions
- Creates healthy habits that build momentum
- Cultivates a sense of control and stability
- Reinforces self-respect by prioritizing your needs daily

How to Create a Routine That Works

Start Small and Be Realistic
Begin with a few key activities that nourish your mind, body, and spirit. This could be morning meditation, journaling, a walk, or setting a daily intention. Avoid overwhelming yourself with too many changes at once.

Anchor Your Routine to Existing Habits
Build new habits by linking them to things you already do. For example, after brushing your teeth, spend five minutes stretching or practicing gratitude.

Include Self-Love Practices
Daily rituals that foster kindness to yourself are essential. This could be positive affirmations, mindful breathing, or simply pausing to appreciate your progress.

Be Flexible and Adapt
Your routine should serve you, not trap you. Life will throw curveballs—adjust your routine as needed, without judgment.

End Your Day with Reflection
Spend a few minutes reviewing what went well and what you want to improve tomorrow. This cultivates awareness and growth.

Sample Morning Routine

- Wake up and drink a glass of water
- Five minutes of deep breathing or meditation
- Write down three things you're grateful for
- Light stretching or gentle movement
- Review your top priorities for the day

The Power of Consistency

Even small, consistent actions compound over time. A daily routine builds discipline, but more importantly, it builds love and respect for yourself by showing up each day with intention.

Practice Gratitude

Gratitude is more than just saying "thank you." It is a deliberate practice of recognizing and appreciating the abundance and blessings in your life — big and small. When you cultivate gratitude, you shift your focus away from what's missing or wrong and open your heart to the richness that already exists.

Practicing gratitude is a powerful tool on your journey to loving yourself more. It nurtures positivity, strengthens resilience, and deepens your connection to yourself and the world around you.

The Science of Gratitude

Research shows that gratitude positively impacts mental, emotional, and physical well-being. People who regularly practice gratitude experience:

- Increased happiness and life satisfaction
- Lower stress and anxiety levels
- Improved relationships and social bonds
- Better sleep and physical health

Gratitude rewires your brain to notice and savor positive experiences, making joy and contentment more accessible.

How Gratitude Enhances Self-Love

When you appreciate what you have and who you are, you build respect and kindness toward yourself. Gratitude helps you:

- Recognize your strengths and achievements
- Accept your imperfections with compassion
- Feel more grounded and peaceful in the present moment

By focusing on abundance rather than scarcity, you reinforce the belief that you are deserving of good things — a foundational pillar of self-love.

Simple Ways to Practice Gratitude Daily

Keep a Gratitude Journal
Each day, write down three things you are grateful for. They can be as simple as a warm cup of tea or a kind word from a friend.

Express Thanks to Others
Make it a habit to verbally thank people who have positively impacted your life, even for small acts of kindness.

Mindful Appreciation
Take moments throughout your day to pause and appreciate the beauty around you — a sunset, a smile, the breath in your lungs.

Reframe Challenges
Try to find a lesson or silver lining in difficult situations, shifting your mindset from victimhood to growth.

Reflection Prompt:

What are three things you are grateful for today? How does focusing on gratitude change how you feel about yourself and your life?

Gratitude is not just for good times — it is a practice to turn to especially when life feels hard. It anchors you, reminding you of the good amidst challenges and helping you maintain hope and resilience.

Chapter 5 Forgive Yourself

Forgiveness is often thought of as something we offer to others—a release granted to those who have wronged us. But one of the most profound and transformative acts of self-love is **forgiving yourself**.

To forgive yourself is to acknowledge your imperfections, your mistakes, and your regrets—not to excuse them, but to free yourself from the heavy burden of guilt and shame. It is an act of compassion that allows healing to begin and opens the door to true growth.

Holding on to past mistakes can keep you trapped in a cycle of self-judgment, doubt, and fear—blocking your path to happiness and success. But when you choose to forgive yourself, you release this weight, reclaim your power, and create space to love yourself more deeply.

In this chapter, we will explore why self-forgiveness is essential, the barriers that often stand in its way, and practical steps you can take to cultivate a forgiving heart. This journey is not always easy, but it is one of the most freeing and loving gifts you can give yourself.

Remember: You are more than your past.
You are worthy of forgiveness—and of the fresh start that comes with it.

Question Your Own Negative Thoughts

Our minds are powerful, but they are not always kind. Negative thoughts often arise uninvited, shaping how we see ourselves and the world around us. These thoughts can be harsh critics, telling us we're not good enough, smart enough, or worthy of love and success. If left unchallenged, they chip away at our confidence and self-respect.

But here's the truth: **Not every thought you have is true.**

Learning to recognize, question, and reframe your negative thoughts is a vital skill on the journey to self-love and happiness. It empowers you to take back control from automatic self-criticism and replace it with more balanced, compassionate perspectives.

Why We Have Negative Thoughts

Negative thinking often stems from past experiences, fears, and deeply ingrained beliefs—sometimes unconscious—that tell us to protect ourselves from failure, rejection, or disappointment. While these thoughts may feel convincing, they do not define who you are.

How to Question Your Negative Thoughts

1. **Become Aware**
   The first step is awareness. Pay attention to when negative thoughts arise. Notice their content, tone, and frequency. Journaling can help capture these thoughts and patterns.
2. **Ask Yourself:**
- *Is this thought based on fact, or just my perception?*
- *Am I catastrophizing or assuming the worst without evidence?*
- *What evidence do I have that supports this thought? What evidence contradicts it?*
- *Would I say this to a friend?*
- *What would I say to myself if I were kind and supportive?*
3. **Reframe the Thought**
   Once you question the negativity, try to reframe it into a more realistic, balanced, or compassionate statement. For example, replace *"I always mess things up"* with *"Sometimes I make mistakes, but I learn and improve."*

4. **Practice Self-Compassion**
   Treat yourself with the same kindness and understanding you would offer others. Negative thoughts often fade when met with gentle compassion rather than harsh judgment.

The Benefits of Challenging Negative Thoughts

- **Improved self-esteem:** When you refuse to accept false negativity, your sense of worth grows.
- **Reduced anxiety and stress:** Questioning catastrophic thoughts calms the mind.
- **Greater emotional resilience:** You develop the ability to bounce back from setbacks without self-criticism.
- **More positive relationships:** When you think kindly of yourself, it reflects in how you connect with others.

A Simple Exercise to Begin

Start by writing down one negative thought you often have about yourself. Then, answer the questions above to challenge it. Finally, write a kinder, more balanced thought to replace it. Repeat this regularly, and over time, you'll notice a shift in your inner dialogue.

Respond to Your Mistakes and Failures with Compassion

Mistakes and failures are an inevitable part of life—no one is immune to them. Yet, how you respond to these moments can either hold you back or propel you forward on your journey of self-love and growth.

Too often, we respond to our missteps with harsh criticism, self-blame, or even shame. This negative self-judgment can erode our confidence, making it harder to try again or believe in ourselves. But there is a more loving and effective way: **respond with compassion.**

Why Compassion Matters

Compassion towards yourself in moments of failure acknowledges your humanity and imperfections without judgment. It's the gentle voice that says, *"I'm learning. I'm growing. This does not define me."*

When you treat yourself with kindness, you create an emotional safe space where healing and resilience can take root. Compassion allows you to reflect on what happened, understand the lessons, and move forward with renewed strength.

How to Practice Self-Compassion After Mistakes

Pause and Breathe
Before reacting with frustration or guilt, take a deep breath. Give yourself a moment to calm your mind and body.

Acknowledge Your Feelings
Allow yourself to feel disappointment, sadness, or frustration—without judgment. Emotions are natural responses, not signs of failure.

Talk to Yourself as You Would to a Friend
Imagine your best friend came to you after a mistake. What kind words would you offer them? Now, say those words to yourself.

Reflect, Don't Ruminate
Instead of replaying the mistake over and over, ask:

- *What can I learn from this?*
- *What will I do differently next time?*
- *How can I be gentle with myself now?*

Practice Forgiveness
Release the grip of self-blame. Remember that everyone

makes mistakes—this moment does not define your worth or potential.

The Growth Mindset

Responding with compassion also means adopting a growth mindset—the belief that abilities and outcomes improve through effort and learning. Mistakes are not dead-ends but stepping stones toward mastery and self-improvement.

Fight Perfectionism with Realistic Thinking

Perfectionism often masquerades as a commitment to excellence, but more often, it becomes a barrier to happiness and progress. It whispers that nothing you do is ever quite good enough, setting impossible standards that lead to frustration, procrastination, and self-doubt.

If you want to love yourself more and attract success and happiness, learning to fight perfectionism with realistic thinking is essential.

Understanding Perfectionism

Perfectionism is the belief that you must be flawless in every area of your life — from your work to your appearance to your relationships. It convinces you that making mistakes is unacceptable, and anything less than perfect is failure.

But this mindset is not only unrealistic; it's harmful. It traps you in a cycle of stress and self-criticism, blocking growth and joy.

How to Develop Realistic Thinking

Set Achievable Standards
Instead of demanding perfection, aim for *progress* and *effort*. Ask yourself, "Is this good enough to move forward?" Remember, done is better than perfect.

Embrace Imperfection as Part of Growth
Accept that mistakes and flaws are natural and valuable teachers. They help you learn, adapt, and improve over time.

Challenge "All-or-Nothing" Thinking
Perfectionism thrives on extremes — either complete

success or total failure. Learn to see the spectrum in between. Small wins count, and partial success is still progress.

Focus on What You Can Control

You can't control every outcome or detail. Direct your energy toward what's realistic and within your reach, rather than striving for impossible standards.

Shifting from perfectionism to realistic thinking frees you from the exhausting pressure of being flawless. It opens the door to creativity, confidence, and authentic joy.

Stop Playing the "I Will Save You" Game

It often begins with good intentions — a desire to help, to fix, to rescue. You see someone struggling, emotionally wounded, or lost in their own chaos, and your instinct is to reach out, to give more than you should, to carry their pain on your shoulders. You believe that your love, support, or presence will be enough to save them. But somewhere along the way, you start losing yourself in the process.

The "I will save you" game is a trap disguised as compassion. It's rooted in the belief that if you love someone hard enough, they will change. That if you give enough, sacrifice enough, or prove your worth, they will finally become the person you need them to be. But real love is not martyrdom. You cannot heal someone who does not want to heal themselves. You cannot sacrifice your peace and call it love.

When you make it your mission to save others, especially at the expense of your own well-being, you're often avoiding something within yourself — the need for control, validation, or a fear of abandonment. You may be using their chaos as a distraction from your own healing.

True self-love means knowing where your responsibility ends and where theirs begins. It means offering love and support without attaching your self-worth to the outcome. It means no longer tying your identity to someone else's progress, pain, or potential.

You are not here to fix people. You are here to *love yourself enough* to stop choosing relationships, friendships, and dynamics where you have to shrink, rescue, or lose yourself just to be seen or valued.

Let them find their own way. Let them rise or fall by their own choices. Your job is to rise for *you*.

Chapter 6 Let go

Letting go is one of the most challenging yet liberating acts you can perform on your journey toward self-love and fulfillment. It requires courage to release what no longer serves you — whether that be painful memories, limiting beliefs, toxic relationships, or unrealistic expectations.

Holding on tightly to past hurts, regrets, or fears can weigh heavily on your heart and mind, blocking your ability to fully embrace the present and create a joyful future. But when you choose to let go, you open space for healing, growth, and new possibilities.

Realize That Your Life Is Made Up of Choices

Every morning, the sun rises, and with it comes a powerful truth: **you have the opportunity to make a new choice.**

Your life is not a fixed script, predetermined by fate or circumstance. Instead, it is a mosaic built one choice at a time—each decision shaping your path, your happiness, and your sense of self-worth. This realization is both humbling and liberating, because it means your future is, in large part, in your hands.

The Power of Choice

Sometimes, when life feels overwhelming or stuck, it's easy to forget this. We may feel like victims of our past, trapped by habits, or confined by other people's expectations. But every day, in small and large ways, you have the power to choose differently.

Choosing how you respond to challenges, how you treat yourself, and which direction you want your life to take is a profound form of self-love. It acknowledges your agency and your ability to create a life aligned with your deepest values and desires.

Every Choice Shapes Your Story

Think of your life as a storybook. Each choice is a new page. Some pages bring joy, others lessons, but all are chapters that contribute to your unique narrative.

- Choosing kindness to yourself over self-criticism nurtures your confidence.
- Choosing to pursue your passions feeds your soul.
- Choosing to forgive releases you from the burdens of the past.
- Choosing to say "no" protects your time and energy.

These choices might seem small in the moment, but collectively, they shape who you become and the life you live.

Embrace Responsibility Without Blame

Owning your choices does not mean blaming yourself for every hardship or mistake. Life's circumstances are complex, and not everything is within your control. But by recognizing where your power lies—in the choices you make—you can move from feeling powerless to empowered.

This mindset invites you to approach life proactively, with curiosity and courage, rather than reacting out of fear or habit.

How to Start Making Conscious Choices

Pause and Reflect: Before reacting automatically, take a moment to consider your options.

Align with Your Values: Choose actions that resonate with what truly matters to you.

Accept Imperfection: Not every choice will be perfect, but each one is an opportunity to learn and grow.

Be Present: Focus on the here and now—your choices today are what shape your tomorrow.

Learn How to Overcome Fears, Failures, and Overthinking

Fear, failure, and overthinking often form a trio that holds many people back from living fully and loving themselves deeply. These challenges can create mental barriers that keep you stuck, doubting your worth, and avoiding risks. But the truth is, **you have the power to break free from this cycle** and move forward with courage and clarity.

Understanding Fear

Fear is a natural response designed to protect us from danger. Yet, in modern life, fear often shows up as anxiety about the unknown or worries about what could go wrong. When fear dominates your mind, it prevents you from taking meaningful steps toward your goals.

How to overcome fear:

- **Name your fear:** Simply acknowledging what you are afraid of can reduce its power.
- **Face it gradually:** Take small steps toward what scares you rather than avoiding it entirely.
- **Shift your focus:** Replace "What if I fail?" with "What if I succeed?" or "What can I learn?"

Reframing Failure

Failure is not the opposite of success—it is a vital part of the journey. Every failure carries lessons that lead to growth and eventual achievement. When you see failure as feedback instead of defeat, you open yourself to resilience and confidence.

How to embrace failure:

- **Change your narrative:** View failures as temporary setbacks, not permanent labels.
- **Analyze and learn:** Ask yourself, "What went wrong? What can I do differently next time?"
- **Celebrate effort:** Recognize your courage for trying, regardless of the outcome.

Calming Overthinking

Overthinking traps you in a loop of worries and doubts, draining your energy and clarity. It often arises when you seek control in uncertain situations, but instead, it clouds your judgment.

How to quiet overthinking:

- **Practice mindfulness:** Focus on the present moment through breathing exercises or meditation.
- **Set time limits:** Give yourself a set time to think about a problem, then move on to action.
- **Challenge catastrophic thoughts:** Ask yourself, "Is this thought realistic? What's the worst-case scenario, and can I handle it?"

Reflection Prompt:

What fear or failure has held you back? What is one small action you can take today to overcome it?

Fear, failure, and overthinking are part of being human, but they don't have to control your life. By learning to face fears, reframe failure, and calm your mind, you reclaim your power and open the door to self-love and success.

Don't Waste Energy Complaining

Complaining often feels like a release — a way to vent frustration, connect with others, or momentarily feel seen. But while it may offer temporary relief, chronic complaining slowly drains your energy and robs you of your power. It shifts your focus from solutions to problems, from gratitude to resentment, from progress to paralysis.

Every time you complain, you're reinforcing the idea that you are helpless — that life is something happening *to* you, rather than something you are actively creating. And the more you give your energy to negativity, the less you have to invest in change, growth, and joy.

Self-love means taking responsibility for your energy. It means choosing to channel your voice toward what empowers rather than what limits. This doesn't mean pretending everything is perfect or suppressing your feelings. It means expressing yourself in ways that are constructive, not destructive. You can acknowledge pain without becoming consumed by it. You can process emotions without broadcasting blame.

Instead of saying, "This always happens to me," ask, "What can I learn from this?"
Instead of "Nothing ever changes," ask, "What one small action can I take today to shift this?"
Instead of focusing on what's missing, honor what's already here.

When you stop complaining, you start creating. You shift from being a passive observer of your life to an active participant. And in that shift, you take your power back — one conscious choice at a time.

Use your energy wisely. Speak words that build, not break. Direct your focus toward solutions, beauty, and growth.

You are not a victim of life. You are the author.

Stop Trying to Keep Up with Everyone

In today's world, it's easy to fall into the trap of comparison — especially when it feels like everyone around you is moving ahead in life while you're stuck or going at a different pace. One common struggle is feeling a lack of self-respect or sadness because you're single while many of your friends are in relationships.

But here's the truth: **your worth is not defined by your relationship status or by how you measure up to others.**

The Comparison Trap

When you constantly compare yourself to others, you overlook your unique journey and the value in your own experiences. Social media often amplifies this feeling, showing only highlight reels of other people's lives, making it seem like everyone else has it all figured out.

But the reality is no one's life is perfect. Behind every happy couple, there are private struggles and imperfections that aren't always visible.

Why You Might Feel Less Than

Feeling "behind" or "incomplete" because you're single can chip away at your self-esteem and respect. You might think:

- *"Why don't I have what they have?"*
- *"Am I missing something?"*
- *"Is there something wrong with me?"*

These thoughts are painful but not true. They come from external pressures and internalized beliefs, not from your actual worth.

Reclaim Your Self-Respect

Honor Your Timeline
Your life unfolds at the right pace for you. Being single is not a deficiency but an opportunity for self-discovery, growth, and freedom.

Focus on Your Own Growth
Invest time in yourself—your passions, goals, and healing. When you build a strong foundation of self-love, you attract healthier relationships naturally.

Shift Your Mindset
Instead of viewing your singleness as a lack, see it as a period rich with potential and self-awareness.

Celebrate Your Wholeness
You are whole and worthy exactly as you are. A relationship can add joy to your life, but it does not complete you.

Self-respect grows when you stop seeking approval from others and start honoring your own feelings and needs.

The moment you stop trying to keep up with everyone else, you reclaim your power and peace.

Distance Yourself from Toxic People

One of the most loving things you can do for yourself is to choose peace over chaos — even when that chaos comes from people you care about.

Toxic people don't always appear harmful at first. Sometimes, they wear the mask of friendship, family, or even love. But over time, you begin to notice the signs: your energy feels drained after spending time with them, your confidence shrinks in their presence, and you start questioning your worth. They manipulate, guilt-trip, criticize, or take without giving. And still, part of you hesitates to walk away, afraid of seeming heartless or selfish.

But protecting your peace is not selfish — it's sacred.

You were not put on this earth to fix people who hurt you. You do not owe loyalty to those who disrespect your boundaries, silence your voice, or make you feel small. Your time, your energy, your love — they are precious. And they must be earned, not demanded.

Distancing yourself from toxic people doesn't mean you're cruel or unforgiving. It means you are choosing to prioritize your mental, emotional, and spiritual well-being. It means refusing to settle for relationships that drain you instead of uplifting you.

You are allowed to walk away from anyone who disrupts your peace — even if they are family. You are allowed to say no, to unfollow, to create space. And in that space, you will breathe easier. You will find clarity. You will begin to hear your own voice again.

Remember: the people you surround yourself with shape the way you see yourself. Choose those who reflect light, not those who dim it.

Have the Courage to Walk Alone

There will be moments on your journey when the path ahead feels quiet — no crowd cheering you on, no hand to hold, no certainty that you're heading in the "right" direction. But sometimes, the most important parts of self-love happen in solitude. Growth, clarity, and healing don't always require an audience — they require courage. The courage to walk alone.

Choosing yourself may mean leaving behind the familiar. It might mean stepping away from relationships, environments, or beliefs that no longer support your evolution. This can feel lonely at first, even painful. But solitude is not the same as emptiness — it is space. Space to hear your own voice. Space to rediscover who you are without the influence of others.

Chapter 7 Take your Power Back

There comes a point in every healing journey when you realize something life-changing: **you don't have to wait for someone else to save you, validate you, or choose you.** You get to choose *yourself*. You get to take your power back.

Maybe you've given too much of yourself to people who didn't see your worth. Maybe you've spent years doubting your potential, hiding your truth, or shrinking to fit someone else's expectations. But those days are over. This chapter is about remembering who you are — and rising.

Taking your power back doesn't mean becoming hard or closed off. It means standing tall in your truth, owning your story, setting boundaries with love, and no longer apologizing for your existence. It means no longer letting fear, guilt, comparison, or past pain dictate your future.

This is your moment to reclaim control — over your emotions, your time, your choices, and your energy. You are not powerless. In fact, you are incredibly powerful when you stop handing that power to everything outside of you.

Identify the Things You Care About

In a world full of noise, demands, and distractions, it's easy to lose touch with what truly matters to you. You may find yourself chasing goals that don't fulfill you or living a life that reflects someone else's expectations. But one of the most empowering acts of self-love is pausing long enough to ask yourself:
What do I truly care about? What makes my soul come alive?

Understanding what you value is not just an exercise in clarity — it's a declaration of identity. It shapes your decisions, builds your confidence, and gives meaning to your journey.

Why This Matters

When you identify what you care about, you create an internal compass. You stop drifting and start choosing.

Instead of saying yes to everything and everyone, you begin aligning your life with what feels genuine to you.

People who live with clarity of values:

- Experience deeper fulfillment
- Make better decisions with less regret
- Cultivate stronger self-respect
- Feel more confident in their identity

Living in alignment with your values helps you trust yourself, which is one of the foundations of self-love.

How to Discover What You Truly Care About

Reflect on What Moves You
Think about the moments that stirred something deep within you. What made you feel inspired, angry, passionate, or alive? These emotions are often clues to your values.

Look at How You Spend Your Time and Energy
Where does your attention naturally go? What activities leave you feeling energized versus drained? Sometimes your priorities are already showing up — they just need to be acknowledged.

Notice What You Stand Up For

What issues or causes do you feel strongly about? What would you defend, protect, or fight for? These are signs of what matters to you at your core.

Consider Who You Admire

The people you respect often reflect qualities or values you hold dear. Ask yourself: *What do I admire about them?* That admiration reveals something about who you are or who you want to become.

Examples of Core Things People Care About

- Creativity and expression
- Freedom and independence
- Family and relationships
- Personal growth and learning
- Honesty and integrity
- Justice and fairness
- Health and well-being
- Faith and spirituality
- Contribution and service

There's no right or wrong list. What matters is that it's *yours.*

Bringing Your Values Into Everyday Life

Once you identify what you care about, ask: *Am I living in alignment with these values?* If not, what small shifts can you make to bring your life into better alignment?

This might mean setting boundaries, changing how you spend your time, or saying no more often. It might even mean reimagining your goals entirely. The important thing is to make choices that reflect who you really are — not who others expect you to be.

Reflect on What Matters Most to You

In the quiet moments — when you're not rushing, performing, or proving — what rises to the surface of your heart? What brings you peace, joy, or a sense of meaning? These are often the answers to a question we don't ask ourselves enough:
What truly matters most to me?

Reflection is powerful because it allows you to reconnect with your inner world — your desires, your boundaries, your passions, and your truth. It slows the noise of the outside world so you can hear the quiet voice of your soul.

In a world that constantly tells you who to be, what to chase, and how to measure your worth, it takes courage to stop and reflect. But it's in this stillness that your deepest values emerge.

Why This Matters

When you don't take time to reflect, you risk living a life of reaction rather than intention. You may end up climbing a ladder that's leaning against the wrong wall — achieving things that don't satisfy your heart or soul.

But when you do pause and ask yourself what matters most, you start living with clarity, purpose, and alignment. Your decisions become rooted in meaning, and your confidence grows because you're honoring your truth.

Journal Questions for Reflection

To help you uncover what matters most, ask yourself:

- What do I want my life to stand for?
- What brings me a sense of peace and fulfillment?
- When have I felt most proud of myself — and why?
- What am I willing to protect, even when it's hard?

- If I had just one year to live, how would I spend it?

Let your answers guide you. Let them shape the way you speak, love, work, and dream.

A Life That Reflects What You Value

The goal isn't perfection. It's alignment.
It's choosing to build a life — relationship by relationship, choice by choice — that reflects what matters most to *you*, not what pleases others or meets society's expectations.

This is how self-love grows: not from performing for the world, but from honoring your truth and letting your values shape your path.

Setting Boundaries — A Radical Act of Self-Respect

For a long time, you may have been taught that being "nice" meant being available, agreeable, and accommodating. That saying *yes* was polite — even when it cost you your peace. That being liked was more important than being true to yourself.

But here's the truth:
Setting boundaries isn't selfish — it's sacred.
It's how you protect your time, your energy, your mental

health, and your self-worth. It's how you teach others how to treat you. And most importantly, it's how you tell yourself, *I matter.*

What Are Boundaries, Really?

Boundaries are the invisible lines that define what is and isn't acceptable in your life. They are limits you set to protect your well-being and create space for what feels aligned.

There are many types:

- **Emotional boundaries** – saying no to conversations that are draining or disrespectful
- **Time boundaries** – choosing not to overcommit or overextend
- **Energetic boundaries** – preserving your space and energy from negativity
- **Physical boundaries** – honoring your body and comfort
- **Digital boundaries** – limiting screen time, notifications, or access to your online presence

When you start to set boundaries, you begin to take your power back — one decision at a time.

How to Know When a Boundary Is Needed

Pay attention to your body and emotions. When you feel:

- Drained after a conversation
- Resentful after saying yes
- Anxious or overwhelmed in certain spaces
- Disrespected, dismissed, or invisible

...those are signals. Your inner self is gently nudging you to draw a line — to protect your peace.

How to Set Boundaries With Confidence and Grace

Get Clear on Your Limits
Ask yourself: What am I no longer available for? What do I need more of in order to feel safe, respected, and whole?

Use Direct, Respectful Language
You don't owe anyone a long explanation. A simple "I'm not available for that," or "That doesn't work for me," is enough.

Expect Resistance
Not everyone will like your boundaries — especially those who benefitted from you not having any. That's okay. Their reaction is not your responsibility.

Stay Consistent
Boundaries lose power when you waver. Hold them with love and strength, even when it's uncomfortable.

Celebrate Yourself
Every time you set a boundary, you reinforce your self-respect. That's something to be proud of.

Affirm This

*"I am allowed to say no without guilt.
I honor my limits with clarity and courage.
I protect my peace, and in doing so, I honor my worth."*

Because you deserve to live a life where you feel safe, seen, and supported. And that starts with the boundaries you set and the love you show yourself.

Recognizing Your Strengths and Talents

There is something powerful within you — something that the world needs, something only *you* can offer.

Yet for so many of us, our strengths and talents often go unrecognized — not because they don't exist, but because we've been conditioned to overlook them. We're taught to focus on what we lack, where we fall short, or how we compare to others. But part of learning to love yourself more is choosing to see and celebrate what already makes you extraordinary.

You Were Born With Gifts

You didn't arrive in this world empty-handed. From the moment you took your first breath, you carried with you the seeds of talent, creativity, empathy, intelligence, and uniqueness. Over time, through experience, struggle, and growth, those gifts evolved into strengths — some of which you may now take for granted.

Maybe you're a natural leader. Maybe you're an incredible listener. Perhaps you create beauty through your hands, or you uplift others simply with your presence. These are not small things — they are *superpowers* when you start to recognize and use them with intention.

Why You May Have Forgotten Your Strengths

You may have been raised in an environment where your gifts weren't nurtured. Perhaps you were taught to be humble to the point of invisibility. Maybe you've been surrounded by people who only pointed out your flaws and never your brilliance.

Or perhaps you've compared yourself so often to others that you began to see yourself through a distorted lens — one that only highlighted what you lacked, rather than what made you shine.

But the truth is: you have strengths. You have talents. And it's time to honor them.

The Importance of Recognizing Your Strengths

Self-love is not just about feeling good about yourself — it's about knowing yourself. And recognizing your strengths helps you:

- Build self-confidence
- Make aligned life and career decisions
- Attract opportunities that match your unique abilities
- Break free from imposter syndrome
- Step into your purpose

You can't fully love yourself if you constantly underestimate yourself. Knowing what you're good at helps you trust your worth, even in a world that sometimes tries to make you forget.

How to Identify Your Strengths and Talents

Here are a few ways to begin uncovering and reclaiming what makes you powerful:

Reflect on Past Wins

What achievements, big or small, are you most proud of? What did you do well in those moments? Look beyond titles or awards. Think about the qualities you brought forward — persistence, creativity, courage, empathy, communication.

Ask Others for Feedback

Sometimes others can see our gifts more clearly than we can. Ask people you trust: *What do you think I'm naturally good at? When have you seen me at my best?* Their answers may surprise you — and validate what you've quietly suspected about yourself.

Notice What Comes Easily to You

Often, our natural talents feel so effortless that we don't even recognize them as "talents." Do people often thank you for your advice, your eye for detail, your writing, or your ability to stay calm under pressure? These are clues.

Follow What Lights You Up

The things that bring you joy are often connected to your strengths. What activities make you lose track of time? What do you *love* to do, even when no one is watching?

Affirming Your Power

Once you've identified your strengths, speak them out loud. Write them down. Affirm them. Claim them without apology. You are not arrogant for recognizing your gifts. You are honoring the truth of who you are.

Here's a simple mantra:

"I am proud of who I am, and I celebrate the gifts that make me unique."

You don't have to be good at everything. You only have to be yourself — and use what you've been given with purpose and confidence.

Reconnect with Your Passions

There was a time when you lit up at the thought of something — maybe painting, writing, dancing, exploring nature, helping others, or simply creating beauty with your hands. These passions weren't about achievement, validation, or making money. They were about joy. They were about *you*.

But somewhere along the way, life happened.

Schedules filled, responsibilities took over, self-doubt crept in. And those passions you once cherished were set aside — perhaps just temporarily, perhaps for so long that you forgot they ever existed.

Yet here's the truth: **what you love deeply is never truly lost.** It waits for you — patiently, quietly — like an old friend, ready to embrace you the moment you choose to return.

Why Passion Matters for Self-Love

Reconnecting with your passions isn't just about fun or self-expression — it's a powerful form of self-love. When you allow yourself to engage in what brings you alive, you're affirming your worth, honoring your essence, and saying: *My joy matters.*

Passion reconnects you with your authenticity. It reminds you of who you were before the world told you who to be. It nourishes your spirit, ignites creativity, and often leads you closer to your purpose.

Signs You've Lost Touch With Your Passion

- You feel unmotivated or emotionally drained.
- Life feels routine or uninspired.
- You struggle to remember what used to bring you joy.
- You've stopped making time for hobbies or creative expression.
- You say, "I'll do it when I have more time" — but time never comes.

These are all gentle signals calling you back to yourself.

How to Reconnect with What You Love

Revisit Your Inner Child

Think back to what you loved as a child. Before the pressure to be productive, what fascinated you? What could you spend hours doing, just for fun?

Create Space for Exploration

Sometimes passion needs a little breathing room to re-emerge. Give yourself time without a goal. Try something new. Return to a hobby without worrying if you're good at it. The key is *presence*, not perfection.

Listen to What Inspires You

What excites you when others talk about it? What kind of content do you naturally gravitate toward? These subtle cues often point to deeper passions you've neglected.

Allow Joy to Be Enough

You don't need to monetize or master your passion. It's enough to enjoy it. In fact, when you let go of pressure, passion flows more freely — and may even open unexpected doors in your life.

Let Passion Lead You Back to Yourself

Reconnecting with your passions is about *remembering* who you are. It's about lighting that internal fire again — not to impress anyone, but because you deserve a life that feels alive.

Passion makes your world feel more vibrant. And when you nurture what lights you up, you begin to glow differently. You become magnetic — not just to others, but to purpose, joy, and alignment.

Final Reflection:
What is something I've always loved, but haven't given myself permission to do lately? What small step can I take this week to reconnect with that passion?

Look for the People You Admire

There's a quiet power in admiration. When you find yourself drawn to someone — their confidence, their creativity, their kindness, or their unapologetic authenticity — you're not just witnessing their light. You're recognizing something familiar. Something you long for. Something, perhaps, that already lives inside of you.

Admiration is a mirror.

It reflects your values, your unspoken dreams, and the version of yourself you're meant to step into. That's why it's important to pay attention to who you admire — not to compare yourself, but to *learn* from them and to *see* yourself in their story.

Admiration vs. Comparison

There's a difference between admiration and comparison.

- **Admiration inspires.** It opens your heart and awakens possibilities. You think, *If she can do it, maybe I can too.*
- **Comparison shrinks you.** It whispers, *She's everything I'm not. I'll never measure up.*

When you catch yourself admiring someone — maybe a public figure, a friend, or even a stranger — pause and shift your focus from jealousy to curiosity. Ask: *What exactly about them moves me?* That answer holds the key to your own growth.

Why the People You Admire Matter

The people you look up to often carry clues about your own inner calling and the kind of life you're meant to lead. Admiration might reveal:

- The values you want to embody
- The lifestyle that resonates with you
- The type of energy you want to carry
- The kind of confidence or creativity you desire to express

Sometimes we admire people not because they are who we want to become exactly, but because they *remind us* of who we really are — beneath the fear, self-doubt, and societal conditioning.

Questions to Ask Yourself

To truly use admiration as a self-love tool, reflect on these questions:

- Who are three people I deeply admire?
- What specific qualities do they possess that I'm drawn to?
- How do those qualities relate to the version of myself I want to become?
- What is one step I can take today to cultivate a similar quality in my own life?

Use Admiration as a Guide, Not a Standard

Admiring someone should never feel like pressure. You're not meant to replicate someone else's journey or personality — you're meant to let their story inspire your *own unique path*.

Let them guide you, not define you. Let their strength or softness remind you of your own. Let their fearlessness be a permission slip for you to be bold in your own way.

And always remember: **If you can see it in someone else, it's because the seed of that same energy already lives within you.**

Surround Yourself with Inspiration

As you grow in self-love, be intentional about who you follow, spend time with, and allow into your mental space. Surround yourself with people — online or in real life — who reflect the kind of energy, grace, and authenticity you want to embody.

Seek mentors, creators, authors, teachers, and even fictional characters who bring out the best in you. Let them be gentle reminders of what's possible. You don't have to know them personally for their presence to be meaningful.

Visualize Your Ideal Self

Close your eyes for a moment.

Now imagine the highest version of you — the woman who wakes up with peace in her heart, speaks with confidence, walks with purpose, and radiates quiet power. She is deeply kind to herself. She honors her boundaries. She doesn't beg to be chosen — she chooses herself, every single day.

That is your **ideal self**.

And she already exists — not in some distant future, but within you right now. She's not a fantasy. She's a *direction*.

Why Visualization Is a Powerful Tool

Your mind is a blueprint-maker. When you regularly *visualize* the life you desire and the version of you who is already living it, your brain starts to rewire itself to believe it's possible. Your thoughts begin to align with your vision, and your actions follow.

Visualization isn't about pretending or escaping reality. It's about anchoring yourself to a clear image of where you're going — emotionally, mentally, spiritually, and even physically.

The clearer the vision, the stronger the pull.

Meet Your Ideal Self

Who is she?

Take a moment to describe her:

- What does she look like, wear, and prioritize?
- How does she speak to herself in the mirror?

- What does her daily routine include?
- How does she respond to setbacks, stress, or failure?
- Who does she surround herself with?
- What lights her up? What does she no longer tolerate?
- What habits has she let go of to protect her peace?

This version of you is not about perfection — it's about alignment. She is you, just more intentional. More self-aware. More rooted in love, not fear.

Bridging the Gap

Once you can *see* her, you can begin to *become* her.

Ask yourself:

- What small choices can I make today that reflect her energy?
- What limiting beliefs do I need to release to align with her?
- What habits support her life — and am I willing to start practicing them?

This isn't about transforming overnight. It's about embodying her in small, meaningful ways — a little more every day.

Start by making decisions she would make. Speak how she would speak. Dress in a way that makes you feel empowered. Set boundaries the way she would. Protect your energy the way she would. Eventually, the gap between who you are and who you envision will begin to shrink — until one day, you'll realize you *are* her.

The Mirror Exercise

Stand in front of a mirror and say:

"I see the woman I'm becoming.
I honor the journey between here and there.
I am her — now, in progress and in power."

Do this daily. Let the image of your ideal self live not only in your mind, but in your reflection, your voice, and your choices.

Journal Prompt:
What does my ideal self look, feel, and live like? What is one step I can take today to embody her energy?

Becoming Her

You made it.
You turned the page, chapter by chapter, and chose to come home to yourself.

This wasn't just a book — it was a mirror, a map, and a permission slip. A mirror to reflect your worth. A map to guide you back to your truth. And a permission slip to love yourself more deeply, more fully, more unapologetically.

Self-love isn't a final destination. It's not a one-time decision. It's a practice. A daily devotion. It's waking up and choosing yourself even when it's hard — especially when it's hard.

Because the truth is, everything begins with you.
The love you give, the boundaries you set, the life you attract — it all stems from how you feel about *you*.

You don't need to be perfect.
You don't need to have it all figured out.
You just need to be present, patient, and willing to rise.

Remember this:

You are allowed to evolve.
You are allowed to take up space.
You are allowed to shine without asking for permission.

The more you love yourself, the more love you will invite.
The more you value your worth, the more valuable your life becomes.
The more you honor who you are, the more magnetic you become to all that is meant for you.

So go ahead — walk boldly into the life your higher self is calling you to.

Because you are not broken.
You are not too late.
You are becoming. And she — the best, brightest, most beautiful version of you — is already within.

All you have to do now is love yourself more.

And never stop.

Printed in Dunstable, United Kingdom